# Giant Squid

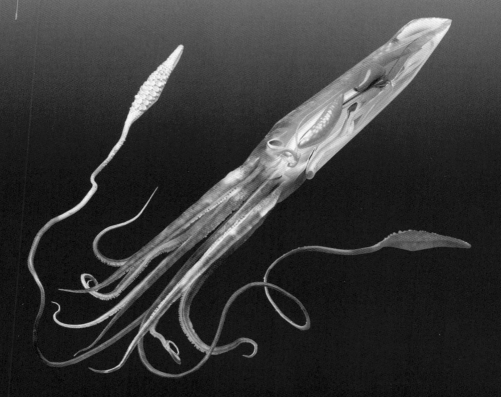

**THIS EDITION**
**Editorial Management** by Oriel Square
**Produced for DK** by WonderLab Group LLC
Jennifer Emmett, Erica Green, Kate Hale, *Founders*

**Editors** Grace Hill Smith, Libby Romero, Maya, Myers, Michaela Weglinski;
**Photography Editors** Kelley Miller, Annette Kiesow, Nicole di Mella; **Managing Editor** Rachel Houghton;
**Designers** Project Design Company; **Researcher** Michelle Harris; **Copy Editor** Lori Merritt;
**Indexer** Connie Binder; **Proofreader** Larry Shea; **Reading Specialist** Dr. Jennifer Albro;
**Curriculum Specialist** Elaine Larson

Published in the United States by DK Publishing
1745 Broadway, 20th Floor, New York, NY 10019

Copyright © 2023 Dorling Kindersley Limited
DK, a Division of Penguin Random House LLC
23 24 25 26 10 9 8 7 6 5 4 3 2 1
001–334110–Sept/2023

A catalog record for this book
is available from the Library of Congress.
HC ISBN: 978-0-7440-7519-9
PB ISBN: 978-0-7440-7520-5

DK books are available at special discounts when purchased in bulk for sales promotions, premiums,
fundraising, or educational use. For details, contact: DK Publishing Special Markets,
1745 Broadway, 20th Floor, New York, NY 10019
SpecialSales@dk.com


Printed and bound in China


The publisher would like to thank the following for their kind permission to reproduce their images:
a=above; c=center; b=below; l=left; r=right; t=top; b/g=background

**Alamy Stock Photo:** Charles Walker Collection 11br, Natural History Museum, London 30,
Science History Images / Photo Researchers 10cl, 10bc, 11tc, WaterFrame_fba 13tr; **BluePlanetArchive.com:** John C. Lewis 12br;
**Stuart Jackson Carter:** 1, 3, 4–5, 8–9, 14–15, 16b, 17t, 18, 19, 20b, 22; **Dreamstime.com:** Ian Dyball 23tr, Daniel Poloha 13,
Yevheniia Ryzhova 10–11, Szefei 20br; **Getty Images:** Archive Photos / Science Source / Photo Researchers History 11cl,
Amanda Nicholls / Stocktrek Images 6bl; **naturepl.com:** Jordi Chias 21; **ORCA:** 26t, 27tl, Dr. Edie Widder & Dr. Nathan Robinson 29

Cover images: *Front:* **Stuart Jackson Carter**


All other images © Dorling Kindersley
For more information see: www.dkimages.com

# For the curious
**www.dk.com**

# Giant Squid

Ruth A. Musgrave

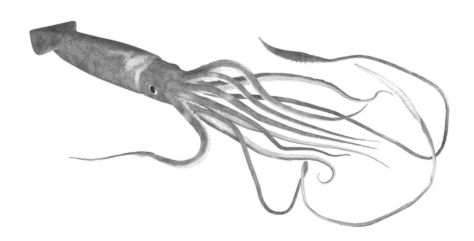

# Contents

**6** Giant Mystery

**8** Supersized

**10** Sea Monster Myths

**12** Little Giants

**14** Grab and Hold

**16** Bizarre Brain

**18** Big Body

**20** Size of the Eyes

**22** Even Bigger Predator

**24** Giant Debate

**26** Meet Medusa

**28** Giant Discovery

**30** Glossary

**31** Index

**32** Quiz

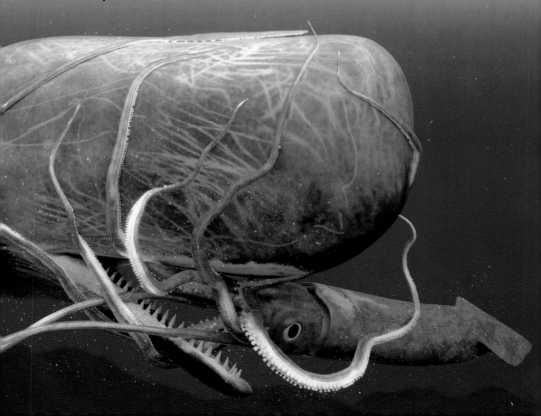

# Giant Mystery

The giant squid moves silently through the water. Its arms and tentacles gracefully curl and stretch. The enormous creature explores the deep sea, looking for something delicious to eat. It watches for predators, too.

Ancient tales portray giant squid as mythical beasts or as deep-sea monsters that attack ships. But these secretive animals are neither. They are a giant mystery. Most of what biologists do know has been learned from studying squid washed up on shore or caught in nets.

### Squid in Charge
These Caribbean reef squid are one of many types of squid. The giant squid's scientific name means "leader of the squids."

The twilight zone is about 650 to 3,300 feet (200 to 1,000 m) from the water's surface.

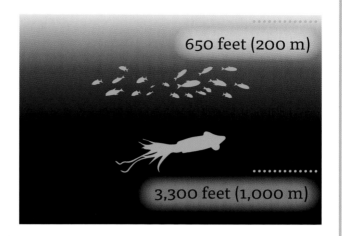

650 feet (200 m)

3,300 feet (1,000 m)

Giant squid live throughout the world, deep in the ocean. They live in the twilight zone. That's where little sunlight penetrates from the water's surface and darkness begins. Giant squid play an important role in their habitat. To learn more, it's important to observe these animals in their home. But that is difficult to do in the dark depths of the ocean.

Deep-sea expert Edith Widder came up with a plan, though. She'd get a giant squid to take a deep-sea video selfie! Let's dive into the dark water to learn a bit more about giant squid.

# Supersized

Any animal that's about as long as a school bus gets to be called giant.

Sensational sea tales of 60-foot (18-m)-long or even longer giant squid abound. But these animals are probably not that huge.

Most reach lengths of 35 feet (11 m) long. The largest recorded giant squid was nearly 43 feet (13 m) long. It would take nine 10-year-old kids lined up head to toe to stretch that long!

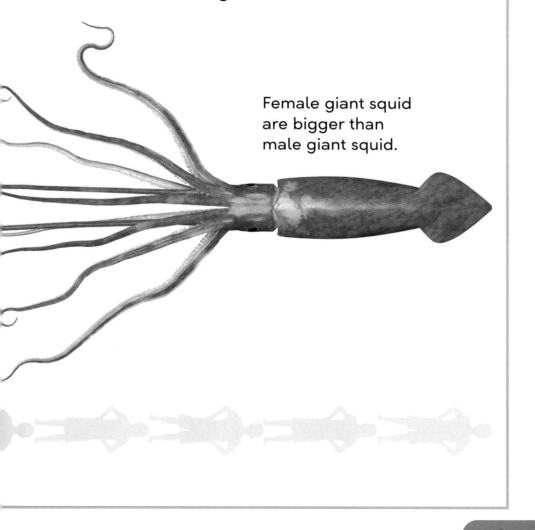

Female giant squid are bigger than male giant squid.

# Sea Monster Myths

For centuries, sailors told tales of monsters sighted in the sea. Some tales were a mix of both science and fiction. These sightings were captured in stories, paintings, poems, and even marked on early maps.

Some tales showed a friendlier version of mythical sea monsters, like this one from the 1600s.

This 16th-century painting shows a sea monster under a ship.

This art from 1573 shows a sea monster as a goose-like creature with scales and fins.

The legend of the Kraken, a giant squid-like creature, has been told for more than 800 years.

The manatee is thought to have inspired tales of mermaids and mermen.

# Little Giants

Baby squid do not start life as giants.

A female lays about a million tiny eggs at a time. Each egg is about the size of three grains of salt placed in a row.

A million eggs is a lot. But most do not survive. Many ocean animals eat the eggs and newly hatched squid.

Those that survive become giant marine predators very quickly. A baby squid grows from smaller than your fingernail to the length of a bus in a couple of years. Compare that to a human's growth. It takes a person about 16 years to reach their adult height.

**Baby Bundle**
This southern calamari squid holds her egg sac in her arms. Biologists think that the female giant squid releases her eggs all at once. The eggs float in a jelly-like mass. When the babies start to hatch, the jelly mass disintegrates.

## Growth Spurt
Other kinds of squid, like this Humboldt squid, also grow incredibly fast, and they only live about one to two years. Some biologists think giant squid might live about five years.

**eggs from one type of squid**

# Grab and Hold

Think of a squid's entire body in three parts: the arms and tentacles, the head, and the mantle.

Giant squid have eight arms. They also have two feeding tentacles, which are twice as long as their arms. The feeding tentacles stretch like elastic to seize prey. The tentacles of a large giant squid can stretch twice as long as the squid's mantle. If a child could do that with her arms, she could tip a basketball in the hoop by just standing on her toes!

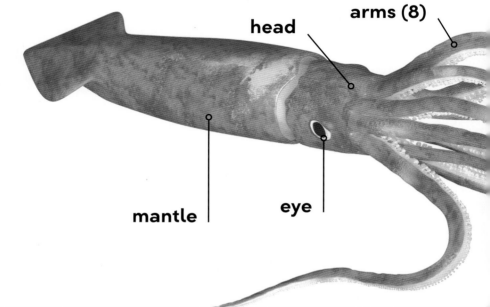

head

arms (8)

mantle

eye

Hundreds of round, sharp suckers line the arms and tentacles. Each sucker has a tooth-like structure around its outside edge. The suckers grip the prey so it cannot escape.

Giant squid eat a variety of fish, crustaceans, and squid, including possibly other giant squid. They use their arms to pull the food to their mouth.

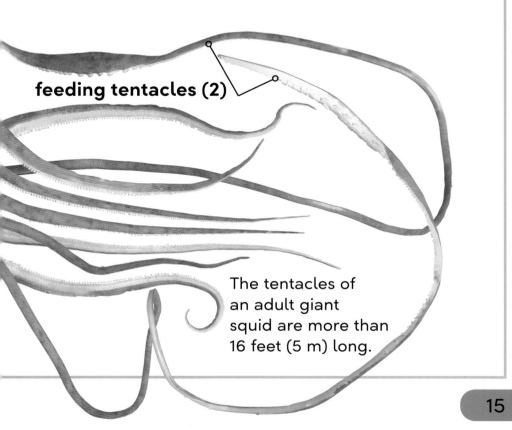

**feeding tentacles (2)**

The tentacles of an adult giant squid are more than 16 feet (5 m) long.

# Bizarre Brain

The squid's head is located between the mantle and its arms. The head includes the brain, mouth, and eyes.

The squid's brain is shaped like a doughnut. There's a reason for that. It has to do with eating.

The squid's mouth and beak are in the center of its arms and tentacles. The beak is razor-sharp. It cuts food into bite-size pieces. The squid's tongue shreds the food into even smaller bits. It's no ordinary tongue. The squid's tongue is covered with small teeth.

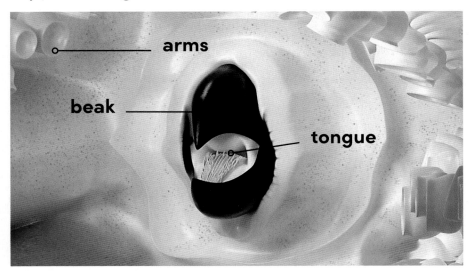

arms

beak

tongue

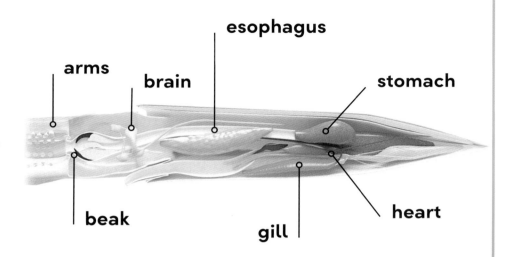

**esophagus**

**arms**

**brain**

**stomach**

**beak**

**gill**

**heart**

The food has to be small before the giant squid swallows it. Giant squid may be big, but they cannot swallow giant bites.

When we swallow, the food travels through a tube from our mouth to our stomach. This is true of a giant squid, too. But the squid has a strange twist. Its brain is between its mouth and stomach. That means the tube that carries the food runs through the center of its doughnut–shaped brain. If a squid swallows something too big, the food can hurt its brain.

# Big Body

The third part of the giant squid's body is the mantle. That's where the internal organs are located. The outside of the mantle is solid but flexible. It has openings near the squid's head. The openings take water into the mantle so the squid can swim and breathe.

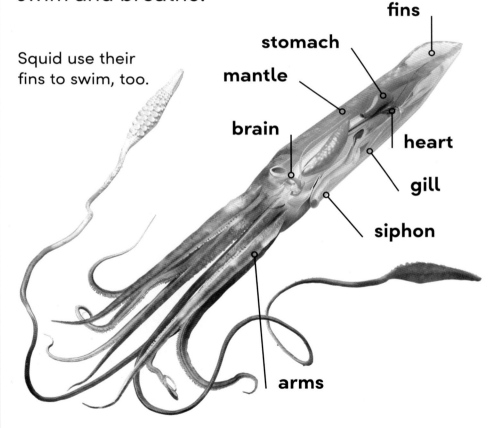

Squid use their fins to swim, too.

fins

stomach

mantle

brain

heart

gill

siphon

arms

**water enters mantle**

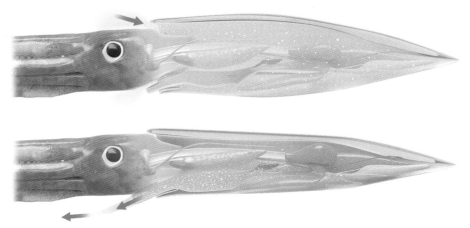

**water is pushed out of siphon**

A tube, called a siphon, connects to the mantle. The squid uses the mantle and siphon to swim. The mantle fills with water. Then, it pumps the water through the siphon. This pushes the squid through the sea.

A giant squid changes directions by turning the siphon. The squid can swim up or down, fins first or tentacles first.

The squid also uses the siphon and mantle to breathe. Water enters the mantle, flows over the gills, and goes out the siphon.

# Size of the Eyes

Giant squid have giant eyes. One eye is bigger than your head. Big eyes are important for the squid to find food and avoid predators.

But what can it see in the dark? Bioluminescent, or glowing, animals. Most animals in the twilight zone glow. They create their own light to find food, avoid predators, and talk to each other.

**Seeing in the Big Sea**
A giant squid's eye can be 12 inches (30 cm) wide.

The atolla jellyfish lives in the deep with giant squid. It uses its bioluminescence like a burglar alarm. When attacked, the jellyfish puts on a dazzling light show. Lights flash and circle around the jellyfish's body.

The light display may attract the attention of bigger predators. One of these predators might swoop in to eat whatever attacked the jellyfish. That gives the atolla a chance to escape.

A giant squid would be attracted to the atolla jellyfish's call for help.

# Even Bigger Predator

Sperm whales hunt giant squid in the twilight zone. A sperm whale can be twice as long as a giant squid.

A sperm whale, shown in this illustration, eats 2,000 pounds (907 kg) of food a day, including giant squid.

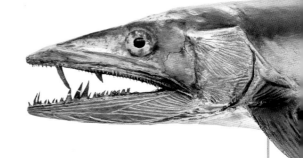

Lancetfish eat smaller giant squid. Lancetfish can be more than seven feet (2 m) long.

When the whales swim through the water, they bump and disturb bioluminescent animals. The motion makes these animals turn on their glow. The giant squid's light-sensitive eyes can see the glowing outline this creates around the whale. This might help them avoid the whales.

The squid don't always escape, but they try. Sperm whales often have round scars caused by the giant squid's sharp suckers.

# Giant Debate

Scientists debate exactly how giant squid hunt. Some think giant squid ambush their prey. The squid floats in the dark and waits for prey to come close enough to grab.

Other biologists think giant squid are active hunters. The squid swims in search of prey and then stalks it to get close enough to grab it.

Some biologists suggest giant squid rely on a sense of smell to find food. Edith Widder and others think those giant eyes play an important role in locating prey.

Video of free-swimming giant squid could give biologists so much information. But giant squid seem wary of submersibles, remotely operated vehicles (ROV),

and other ocean exploration machines.
They might avoid them because of the
noise, vibrations, and bright white lights.
Widder thought of a way to attract a
squid and not have the equipment
scare it away.

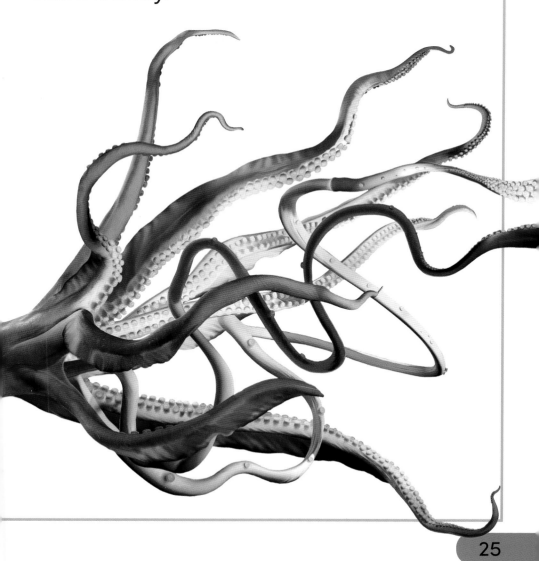

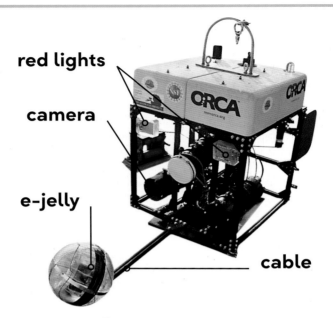

red lights

camera

e-jelly

cable

# Meet Medusa

Widder and her colleagues invented a piece of research equipment called the Medusa. Unlike submersibles and ROVs, the Medusa is quiet. That's because it does not have an engine. It is connected to a ship by a cable. Then, it's lowered deep into the sea, where it floats.

The Medusa also has a special underwater camera system that can film in the dark just using red light. Most deep-sea animals cannot see the color red, so the red lights do

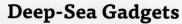

not scare the animals or hurt their eyes. But the Medusa had to do more than just float quietly and film. It had to get the squid's attention.

Widder decided to copy the atolla jellyfish. She created an electronic jellyfish called an e-jelly to mimic the color and pattern of the atolla's burglar alarm.

Then, she and a team of marine biologists took the Medusa out to sea.

**Big Ocean, Little Machines**
The ocean is huge. Submersibles and ROVs are small. Think of trying to explore the entire world at night in a small car. That's what it is like to explore the sea with a submersible or ROV.

# Giant Discovery

The Medusa quietly floated in the deep, its camera ready, the e-jelly flickering. Widder and the team waited aboard the ship. But not for long.

First, a shadow. Then, the giant squid's body, as the animal moved closer. It was stalking the e-jelly! It came closer and then moved farther away. It moved its arms and tentacles up and down as it tracked the e-jelly's movement.

One arm reached out to touch the Medusa. Then, the giant squid wrapped more arms around it to get close to the e-jelly. When it realized the e-jelly wasn't food, it quickly slipped into the darkness.

Widder's research plan had worked. After decades of trying to see a giant squid in the deep, scientists caught a glimpse.

The Medusa's video also answered some of their questions about how giant squid hunt. It showed that giant squid are active hunters, attracted to bioluminescent light.

There is still so much to learn. What would you invent to discover more about giant squid?

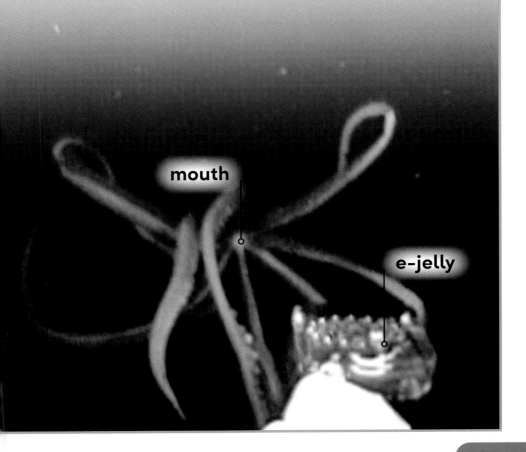

mouth

e-jelly

# Glossary

**Crustaceans**
Animals such as shrimp, crabs, and lobsters that have a hard outer skeleton

**Esophagus**
The tube that carries food from the mouth to the stomach

**Marine biologist**
A scientist that studies the ocean and ocean animals

**Predator**
An animal that eats other animals

**Prey**
An animal that is eaten by other animals

**Remotely operated vehicle (ROV)**
An ocean exploration machine that people pilot from a ship

**Siphon**
A short tube connected to a squid's mantle that helps the animal breathe and move through the water

**Submersible**
An ocean exploration vessel scientists ride inside to explore the deep sea

**Twilight zone**
A "layer" of the ocean that is 650 to 3,300 feet (200 to 1,000 m) from the water's surface

**giant squid tentacle with suckers**

# Index

arms   14–15, 16, 17, 18, 28

atolla jellyfish   21, 27

baby squid   12

beak   16, 17, 18

bioluminescence   20–21, 23, 29

body parts   14–19

brain   16–17, 18

breathing   18, 19

camera   26–28

e-jelly   27–28

eggs   12

esophagus   17

eyes   14, 20–21, 23

feeding tentacles   15

fins   19

food   15–17

gills   17, 18, 19

growth   12–13

head   14, 16

hearts   17, 18

hunting   24–25, 29

jellyfish   21, 27

lancetfish   23

life span   13

mantle   14, 18–19

Medusa   26–29

mouth   16, 17

myths   10–11

remotely operated vehicle (ROV)   24, 27

sea monster myths   10–11

selfies   7

siphon   18, 19

size   8–9, 20–21

sperm whales   22–23

stomach   17, 18

submersibles   24, 27

suckers   15

swimming   18, 19

tentacles   14–15, 16, 19, 28

tongue   16

twilight zone   7, 20, 22

whales   22–23

Widder, Edith   7, 24–28

# Quiz

Answer the questions to see what you have learned. Check your answers in the key below.

1. Why does the giant squid have big eyes?

2. What do giant squid eat?

3. How many arms does a squid have?

4. What does a squid use its tentacles for?

5. How did the scientists get the giant squid's attention?

6. What animal did the e-jelly mimic?

7. What is between the squid's mouth and stomach?

8. Where do giant squid live?

1. To look for prey and predators  2. Fish, crustaceans, and squid
3. Eight  4. To catch prey  5. They invented the e-jelly to attract
giant squid  6. Atolla jellyfish  7. The brain  8. In the twilight zone